The Easy Guide to Shofar Sounding

Arthur L. Finkle, R.J.E.

Torah Aura Productions

ISBN #1-891662-22-8

© 2002 Arthur J. Finkle

Published by Torah Aura Productions

Torah Aura Productions
4423 Fruitland Avenue
Los Angeles, California 90058
(800) BE-TORAH • (323) 585-7312
fax (323) 585-0327

MANUFACTURED IN THE UNITED STATES OF AMERICA

To my beloved Linda, Andrew & Daniel
and to my rebbe, Rabbi Jack Pianko

THE SOUNDING OF THE SHOFAR HAS BECOME A VERY EMOTIONAL AND SPIRITUAL EVENT FOR MANY CONGREGANTS. This strident and strange sound (like a whale's or dolphin's whelp) from this very ancient instrument bestirs the soul and moves the congregants to repentance. "The shofar has the quality to stir the hearts and to inspire love, as it is written: 'Shall a shofar be blown in a city and the people not tremble'" (Amos 3:6).

Many congregants become interested in sounding the shofar themselves. What follows is intended to be read before Rosh ha-Shanah and Yom Kippur (the period of repentance and atonement). It will attempt to help those who sound the shofar (not an impossible task) as well as to develop an appreciation of this ancient instrument.

The shofar is the only musical instrument of ancient Israel that survived two millennia in its original form and is still used today.

5

Unlike some of the other instruments of the Temple period, the shofar was uniquely semitic. The word "shofar" is derived from the Assyrian *shapparu*, a wild goat of the ibex family.

Medieval philosophers and mystics have attributed certain moralizing and occult meanings to the sounding of the shofar. Rabbi Saadia Gaon (10th century) stated that the sound of the shofar raised awe and emotion in the hearts and souls of the people. Maimonides interpreted the sounding as reminding humankind of its duties to God. The mystical Zohar holds that the sound of the shofar awakens the Higher Mercy.

The shofar is the most-mentioned instrument in the Bible (72 times). It held a special religious and secular role in the life of the Jewish people. Only Priests and Levites were allowed to perform the religious function of blowing the shofar in the Jewish Commonwealth.

The shofar had several religious roles recorded in the *TaNaKH* (the Bible), such as the transfer of the Ark of the Covenant (2 Samuel 6:15; 1 Chronicles 15:28); the announcement of the New Moon (Psalms 81:4); the beginning of the religious New Year (Numbers 29:1); the Day of Atonement (Leviticus 25:9); the procession preparatory to the Feast of Tabernacles (Mishnah, *Hullin* 1:7); the libation ceremony (Mishnah, R.H.

4:9); and the Havdalah ceremony marking the end of a festival (Mishnah, _Hullin_ 1:7).

In addition, the shofar had a number of secular roles, such as coronating a king (2Samuel 5:10; 1 Kings 1:34; 2 Kings 1;13) and signaling in times of war to assemble troops, to attack, to pursue, and to proclaim victory (Numbers 10:9, Judges 6:4; Jeremiah 4:5 and Ezekiel 33:3-6).

In post-biblical times, the shofar was enhanced in its religious use because of the ban on playing musical instruments as a sign of mourning for the destruction of the Temple. (It should be noted that a full orchestra played in the Temple, including, perhaps, a primitive organ.) The shofar continues to announce the new year and the New Moon, to introduce the Sabbath, and to carry out the commandments on Rosh ha-Shanah and Yom Kippur. The secular uses have been discarded (although the shofar was sounded to commemorate the reunification of Jerusalem in 1967) (Judith Kaplan Eisendrath, _Heritage of Music_, New York: U.A.H.C., 1972, pp. 44-45).

It is a positive commandment from the Torah to hear the sounding of the shofar on Rosh ha-Shanah, as Numbers 29:1 teaches: "It should be a day of sounding the shofar for you."

Mishnah Torah
Laws of Shofar 1.1

Rosh ha-Shanah

THE SHOFAR IS PRIMARILY ASSOCIATED WITH ROSH HA-SHANAH. Indeed, Rosh ha-Shanah is called *Yom T'ru'ah* (the day of the shofar blast). In the Mishnah (book of early Rabbinic laws derived from the Torah), a discussion centers around the centrality of the shofar in the time before the destruction of the Second Temple (70 C.E.). Indeed, the shofar was the center of the ceremony, with two silver trumpets playing a lesser role. On other solemn holidays, fasts, and New Moon celebrations, two silver trumpets were featured, with one shofar playing a lesser role. The shofar is also associated with the Jubilee Year in which, every fifty years, Jewish Law provided for the release of all slaves, land, and debts. The sound of the shofar on Yom Kippur proclaimed the Jubilee Year that provided the actual release of financial encumbrances.

Halakhah (Jewish Law) rules that the shofar may not be sounded on the Sabbath due to the potential that the *Ba'al T'kiyah* (Shofar Sounder) may inadvertently carry it, which is in a class of forbidden Sabbath work. (R.H. 29b) The historical explanation is that in ancient Israel, the shofar was sounded on the

8

Sabbat in the Temple located in Jerusalem. After the Temple's destruction, the sounding of the shofar on the Sabbath was restricted to the place where the Great Sanhedrin (Jewish legislature and Court from 400 B.C.E. to 100 C.E.) was located. However, when the Sanhedrin ceased to exist, the sounding of the shofar on the Sabbath was discontinued (Kieval, *The High Holy Days*, p. 114).

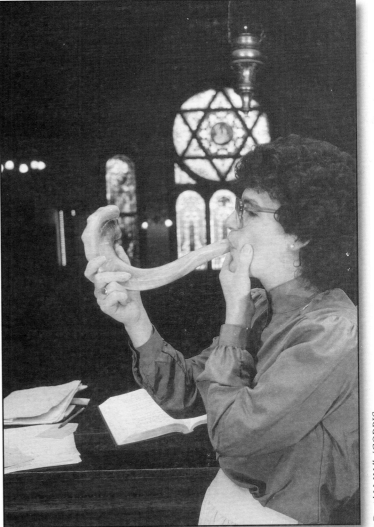

Ba'al T'kiyah

BEING A *BA'AL T'KIYAH* (SHOFAR SOUNDER) IS AN HONOR. "The one who blows the shofar on Rosh ha-Shanah...should

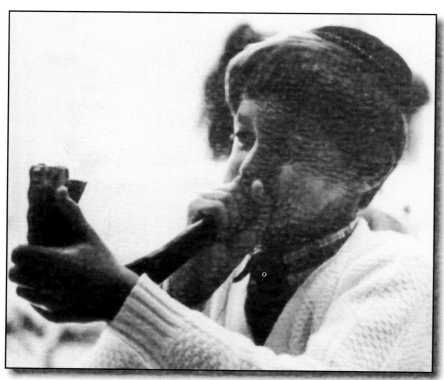

likewise be learned in the Torah and shall be God-fearing, the best man available. However, every Jew is eligible for any sacred office, providing he is acceptable to the congregation. If, however, he sees that his choice will cause dissension, he should withdraw his candidacy, even if the improper person will be chosen" (*Shulḥan Arukh* 3:72). The *Ba'al T'kiyah* shall abstain from anything that may cause ritual contamination for three days before Rosh ha-Shanah (*Shulḥan Arukh* 3:73).

When I train Shofar Sounders, I make sure that they all participate in the service and that no one is highlighted at the expense of another. I have also declined invitations to sound the shofar at other congregations if I know that I will displace another sounder. The democracy of each congregation is important. And it only enhances a sense of participation of as many people as possible can participate in a service.

Finally, the *Ba'al T'kiyah* shall recite the benedictions before the shofar ceremony.

The sound of the shofar reminds us of the trumpet blasts which announce the coronation of a ruler. On Rosh ha-Shanah, God created the world and became its sovereign. By sounding the shofar, we acknowledge God as our ruler.

Abudraham 22:69

The Physical Shofar

Rosh ha-Shanah is the first of the Ten days of Repentence. The shofar is sounded to stir our consciences, urging us to confront our errors and return to God.

Abudraham 22:69

SHOFARS ARE MADE OF HOLLOWED-OUT ANIMAL HORNS, NO TWO OF WHICH ARE ALIKE. In order to be ritually correct, the shofar must be made of any domestic animal's horn except a cow's because of the association with the Golden Calf episode (R.H. 3:2). The accepted Ashkenazic (European) practice is to use a ram's horn, which reminds the participants of the Bible passage in which Abraham almost sacrificed Isaac. However, after God interrupted this heart-rending deed, Abraham instead sacrificed a ram whose horns were caught in a bush. (This Torah portion is read on Rosh ha-Shanah.) The Sephardim (North African, Arabian, and Turkish Jews) customarily use the large horn of a mountain goat or ibex.

The shofar must be curved in shape to symbolize the bent and humbled spirit appropriate for Rosh ha-Shanah (R.H. 26b). The inside of the shofar may not be painted or decorated with carved designs or with gold. However, the outside of the shofar may be decorated or overlaid with gold (as was done at the Temple) as long as the mouthpiece is not covered and the natural tone of the shofar is not changed (R.H. 3:3). There are also laws about usage of a shofar that is cracked or otherwise blemished.

The shofar is somewhat like a trumpet but does not have anything approaching the mathematical precision of its construction. Because no two animals are exactly alike, each shofar is different. In addition, shofars are roughly cut, imperfectly shaped, and of varying thickness.

Like the trumpet, a shofar has a mouthpiece that is shaped when the horn is soft. (It is boiled first to extract the inside tissue.) However, again there is none of the mathematical precision that is found in the trumpet. To find a shofar that has a nearly correct relation is sheer luck (Albert Kramer, *Secrets of a Shofar Blower*, Washington, D.C.: Casilla's Press, 1971, pp. 3-12).

© Ted Spiegel/CORBIS

13

Choosing a Shofar

© Richard T. Nowitz/CORBIS

IN SELECTING A SHOFAR, IT IS CRITICAL TO SOUND ALL THE SHOFARS THAT ARE AVAILABLE BECAUSE THE EASIER THE RELATIONSHIP OF YOUR EMBOUCHURE (LIP MUSCULATURE) TO THE UNIQUENESS OF THE SHOFAR, THE BETTER. The primary interest is in the quality of the tone and the ease with which it is achieved. Almost any hollow tube can be made to produce a sound. But the sound desired is the true tone unique to the shofar. A perfect shofar cannot really be found because its rough method of construction results in many flaws.

Even with a shofar that seems to be satisfactory, the chances are that after it is blown for a moderate length of time, the warmth of the breath will warp it somewhat. The hope is that a shofar will expand and contract reasonably evenly in all directions with changes in temperature so as not to throw it out of tune. Of course, this is typical with most musical instruments; pitch is always subject to correction. Since the custom is to conceal the shofar before it is played, the best method of concealment is to keep it near the body between the armpit and the chest and underneath a jacket, thereby concealing the shofar and keeping it at body temperature.

The sound of the shofar reminds us of the call of the prophets whose voices rang out like a shofar denouncing wrongdoing and calling people to serve God and each other.

Abudraham 22:69

Care of the Shofar

THE CARE OF THE SHOFAR IS IMPORTANT FOR BOTH ASSURING TONALITY AND PRESERVING THE INSTRUMENT ITSELF. The shofar is conventionally cleansed with vinegar. But this isunsatisfactory. Although our ancestors probably thought that vinegar was a good antiseptic, it is not. Vinegar is a dilute solution of acetic acid. It is 95% water. Water has a hydration effect on the inside wall of the shofar. The hard material of a shofar is made essentially of a hard, globular keratin protein (related to hoof, hair, skin, claws, and fingernails). A manicurist, for example, softens fingernails by placing them in a dish of water. A similar softening effect takes place on the inside wall when vinegar is put into the shofar, and the soft horn walls deaden the sound.

The horn of the animal is made hollow by cleaning out the marrow, blood, and cords. It is usually not possible to clean it out completely. The stringy parts left behind throw off an offensive odor, especially when the parts come into contact with vinegar.

A much superior way of keeping the shofar clean is by the use of alcohol. Ordinary rubbing alcohol, either ethyl or isopropyl, is satisfactory. Both are highly antiseptic and have the further

The shofar reminds us of the destruction of the Temple and calls us to take a part in Israel's renewal.

16

advantage of drying quickly and completely which vinegar does not. You can obtain a very quick drying by placing the shofar, after running alcohol through it, over the outlet grille of a room air-conditioning unit. A hairdryer works as well.

The shofar reminds us of the ram offered by Abraham instead of Isaac. It therefore reminds us of the heroic faith of our ancestors.

Abudraham 22:69

Sounding the Shofar

To produce a sound on the shofar, it is necessary to vibrate the air inside of it by placing the horn against the corner of the mouth and by vibrating the lips, which induces vibrations of the air.

Air is an elastic medium in which waves can be reproduced by alternately compressing and rarefying it. Each lip should cover a part, preferably half, of the opening. If the lips are relaxed, they will vibrate and produce sound as the air passes through the horn. A minimum of 16 vibrations per second is necessary to produce sound audible to the human ear. The tauter the lips, the higher the sound pitch.

Contrary to popular belief, it is not a strain to blow the shofar. The effort required is relatively slight in vibrating the lips. In fact, perfecting a decent sound from a French horn or trumpet is much more difficult. In addition, there are no fingering techniques to learn. A shofar is like a primitive bugle.

The shofar is a reminder of the day of final judgment calling upon all people and all nations to prepare for God's judgment.

Abudraham 22:69

The Ritual Sounds

THERE ARE THREE SOUNDS OF THE SHOFAR, NAMELY:

1. *T'kiyah*
2. *Sh'varim*
3. *T'ru'ah*

A fourth sound, *T'kiyah G'dolah* (Great *T'kiyah*), is simply a prolonged *T'kiyah*. Each note shall be equivalent in time to each other (R.H. 34:9).

There is a difference of opinion in the Talmud as to whether the *Sh'varim* or the *T'ru'ah* were sounded at the Temple. The Rabbis compromised and codified both notes as valid. They also pronounced the *Sh'varim-T'ru'ah* together when these notes came in sequence, in order to show this compromise. (R.H. 4:9)

There are also regional (Lithuanian, Hungarian, Sephardic, etc.) differences regarding the exact notes sounded for the different sounds. The following section is based on the system I use.

The *T'kiyah* note starts out as a low note, near the fundamental tone of the shofar; then it rises quickly about three notes in

The shofar foreshadows the proclamation of freedom when the exiled and homeless of Israel will return to their land.

the diatonic scale. Finally, it proceeds to a full octave above the first note. This may be diagrammed as follows:

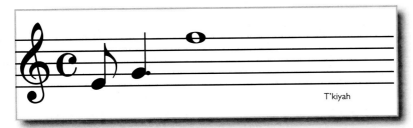

The higher notes are obtained by tightening the lips.

The *Sh'varim* consists of the short blasts, each one third the duration of the *T'kiyah.*

The shofar foreshadows a time when all people will acknowledge that God is One.

Abudraham 22:69

The *T'ru'ah* is simply nine staccato notes sounded in rapid succession. Again, the duration is one ninth that of the *T'kiyah*. To correctly render the *T'ru'ah*, it is necessary to accent the last note. There is also another school that accents the last note and takes the note up a third. The *T'ru'ah* is:

T'ruah

T'kiyah G'dolah is a long *T'kiyah*, "as long as you can hold it."

T'kiyah G'dolah

The shofar must not be sounded with any other musical instrument, such as those in an orchestra, or even another shofar. Also, it must not be seen before it is blown. It must not be heard by reproduction; the sound must reach the ear directly from the shofar without any intervention. Thus, hearing a shofar over the radio or TV is not valid. A deaf person cannot hear the sound, and

© Bettmann/CORBIS

thus cannot fulfill the commandment. The benedictions recited before the shofar is sounded must be recited by the *Ba'al T'kiyah* and no one else. Traditionally, the Shofar Sounder wears a kittel (prayer gown) and may cover his head with his prayer shawl to commune with God.

Ba'al T'kiyah's Preparation

THE *SHULḤAN ARUKH* (128:8) INSTRUCTS THAT THE SHOFAR SHALL BE SOUNDED IN THE PERIOD BETWEEN *ROSH ḤODESH* (NEW MONTH) *ELUL* UNTIL AFTER YOM KIPPUR. The religious rationale was that Moses ascended Mount Sinai to receive the second tablets, dwelt there for 40 days, and descended on the tenth of *Tishre,* when the atonement was completed. The musical rationale is that the forty-day period provided the necessary practice to develop the appropriate embouchure.

The *Ba'al T'kiyah* should get acquainted with the shofar's sounds. He or she (this is not the place to discuss the halakhah of a female's participation in the shofar ritual) should practice the three true notes as long as possible without playing the phrases in order to build the embouchure and to become familiar with the shofar's pitch. This practice should continue for a week to ten days for ten to twenty minutes a day. (There is more practice to do for a first-time *Ba'al T'kiyah.*) Always play standing up, as if it were an actual playing, because when you sit down, a slight tilt of the mouthpiece occurs and will ruin the optimum embouchure. (Take it from one who knows.)

In the second week, the *Ba'al T'kiyah* should practice the three phrases. For the *T'kiyah*, there is a slurring of three notes. The middle note is the most important to reach, as a miscue will not be noticed if the first and third notes are missed. The *Sh'varim* is probably the most difficult, because there is a slurring beginning with the distinct low note. Make sure that this low note is sufficiently prominent by extending this note as long as possible. Incidently, I have found that this extended low note is the most difficult for me to perfect. The *T'ru'ah* is a sound of nine staccato blasts.

The Holy One Who is to be Blessed said: "So will your children become entangled in many kinds of sins and trapped in many kingdoms. But in the end they will be redeemed by the sound of the shofar."

Sefer ha-Aggadah 3: 45

The *T'kiyah G'dolah* is an elongated *T'kiyah*. Hold it as long as you are able. You should be able to hold it for 30-40 seconds with the proper breathing from the diaphragm and chest cavity as any wind instrumentalist will tell you. When you have developed your embouchure sufficiently well, it is possible to elongate the third note as well as the second. This end flourish is dramatic. Which brings me to an often-asked question: "How long should you hold the last note (*T'kiyah G'dolah*)?" Many people feel self-conscious about holding the note too long so as to seem to show off. My answer is rooted in the Mishnah, R.H. 3:3, which indicates that the duty of the day (Rosh ha-Shanah) falls on the shofar. Therefore, Rosh ha-Shanah is associated with the shofar. Thus, the more emphasis on the shofar, the better. Consequently, the longer the blast, the better. (One of my pupils has achieved 65 seconds!)

Another frequently asked question is how to make the note clear in the beginning. In music, we must "attack" the note to accent the clarity of the note. A good technique is to silently say "tu" when the tongue touches the top of the mouthpiece and the upper lip in order to sound the note.

If your lips get tired, allow your lips to relax, and then vibrate them, which allows blood to circulate to the overextended lip. It also helps to support the bottom lip with your fingers. But the best remedy is to practice sufficiently so that your lips will be able to withstand the muscular effort of vibrating.

If your shofar "gurgles," you have spittle in the horn. The best remedy is to use a coffeepot brush to remove the spittle. In fact, after each section of the service in which the shofar is sounded, you should clean out the shofar to avoid this problem. Before you sound the shofar at all, you should clean the shofar with ethyl alcohol.

You should also keep in mind what to do when your note comes out incorrectly. It is better to know what to do before you err rather than panic when the error occurs (and believe me, everybody has erred on the shofar). If your notes are not exact,

The sounding of the shofar should still function in the life of the Jewish people, as an invitation to the individual Jew to review his oath of those ideals, the realization of which would convert human society into God's empire.

Mordechai Kaplan

27

ignore the mistake and go on to the next note. If you blow and nothing comes out, stop the attempt, and place the mouthpiece on a different place on the lips. If you still persist, aim for the fundamental note and just sound it with no other notes. When the lips are used to the vibrations, you can sound the other notes.

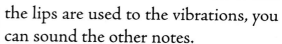

Only play one shofar, because each shofar requires a different embouchure. Thus, for the once or twice a year that you play the shofar, it is foolhardy to change the fixed embouchure that has been formed by sounding your special shofar.

At times, you will find that the keratin will crack, causing the notes to vary. If so, the Mishnah allows you to use the shofar by plugging up the hole. If the hole is horizontal and if there is an unbroken space of two fingers from the beginning of the mouthpiece and the space of two fingers from the break to the end of the shofar, you may repair it by putting some tape over it. Once I used a clarinet filler (some kind of resin), but the tone was never the same. And if the

28

sound is not the same, then it is unkosher (R.H. 3:6). If the horn is not kosher, you may feel comfortable with a new shofar whose mouthpiece matches your embouchure.

Always protect the mouthpiece. Put a cushion around it so that if the shofar falls, the mouthpiece will not chip. If it does, the chances are that it will not be repairable.

If it is possible, one-half hour before playing, you should practice for five minutes to warm up.

The Holy One Who is to be Blessed said, "My children, if your deeds improve, I will treat you like a shofar. Just as you blow into one end of the shofar and the sound comes out the other, so I will rise from the throne of law and will sit on the throne of mercy.

Lev. R. 26:6

Time and Place

THE SHOFAR IS SOUNDED AT THE END OF THE TORAH SERVICE ON THE BIMAH (PULPIT) WHERE THE TORAH IS READ (OREKH HAYYIM, 585.1). It is also sounded three times in the additional service (the Malkhuyyot, the Zikhronot, and the Shofarot).

In European *Maḥzorim* (High Holy Day Prayerbooks), the *Ba'al T'kiyah* sounds 100 notes after the Torah service: 30 notes each for the three divisions of the additional service. Then the *Ba'al T'kiyah* sounds ten more notes at the *Titkabel Kaddish*.

The traditional custom in the United States is to sound 100 notes (30 immediately after the Torah service, 10 each after the three divisions of the additional service). The remaining 40 notes are completed by sounding 30 notes at the *Titkabel Kaddish* and 10 notes after the Mourner's Kaddish.

In Closing

In closing, the Shofar Sounder who performs the present-day commandments is carrying on an ancient tradition. The shofar sounder stands in the footsteps of the holy priests, the great warriors, the talmudic sages, the great editors, and the great philosophers. Indeed, the shofar represents the mystery of the survival of the Jewish people.

© Jonathan Torgovnik/CORBIS

Explanatory Notes

Kaddish: A prayer of praise to God. The service contains five variations of this prayer.

Maimonides: A Jewish teacher, Rabbi, philosopher and physician, Maimonides (also known as Rambam) lived from 1135 to 1235. His *Mishne Torah* is a major work that interprets Jewish theology in the Western idiom. He also served as a personal physician to Saladin the Great, Sultan of Egypt and Syria.

Mishnah: A compilation of Jewish Law derived from interpretation of the Hebrew Scriptures. There are 63 tractates in the Mishnah.

Orekh Hayyim: One of the four sections of the Shulhan Arukh (see below).

R.H. X:X: The tractate Rosh ha-Shanah from the Mishnah, a compilation of Rabbinic Law codified by Rabbi Judah in 200 C.E.

R.H. 23a: The tractate Rosh ha-Shanah from the Talmud, a compilation of Rabbinic Law codified in 525 C.E. and later commented on by other Rabbinic authorities.

Saadia Gaon: The greatest Rabbinic authority of the early medieval period, Saadia was head of the Pumbedita Yeshiva. His *Emunah V'deyot* is one of the most important works in Jewish philosophy. He lived from 882 to 942 C.E.

Shulhan Arukh: The standard Code of Jewish Law compiled and published by Rabbi Yosef Caro (1488–1575).

Tanakh: The Torah (5 books of Moses), the N'vi'im, (Prophets) and the K'tuvim (Writings).